P9-DMS-396

digging in the dirt

A Kid's Guide to How Herbs Grow

Patricia Ayers

The Rosen Publishing Group's
PowerKids Press™
New York

Published in 2000 by The Rosen Publishing Group, Inc.
29 East 21st Street, New York, NY 10010

First Edition

Book Design: Maria Melendez

Photo Credits: Cover and title page, pp. 1, 5, 6, 7, 9, 14, 20 © Tony Stone Images; p. 8 © Super Stock; p. 10 © International Stock.

Photo Illustrations: pp. 1, 4, 11, 12, 15, 16, 17, 22 © Donna Scholl.

Ayers, Patricia.
        A Kid's guide to how herbs grow / by Patricia Ayers.
        p. cm. — (Digging in the dirt)
    SUMMARY: Follows a school class as they learn about different kinds of herbs and plant and care for their own herb garden.
    ISBN 0-8239-5464-1 (lib.bdg.)
    1. Herb gardening Juvenile literature. 2. Herbs Juvenile literature. [1. Herbs. 2. Herb gardening. 3. Gardening.] I. Title. II. Series:
Ayers, Patricia. Digging in the dirt series.
    SB351.H5 A94 1999
    635'.7—dc21

                                                                                            99-28911
                                                                                            CIP

Manufactured in the United States of America

Contents

Herbs Have a History

Would you like to feel a leaf that is as soft as rabbit fur and smells like gum? If so, rub the leaves of the peppermint-scented *geranium*. *Geranium* is an herb. **Herbs** are plants that are used for a special purpose. Many herbs make food taste better. Some, like *geranium*, can make clothes and rooms smell nice. Other herbs are used to make dyes, bug sprays, and soaps. For thousands of years people used herbs as medicines for almost every illness. Sometimes the herbs worked and sometimes they didn't. People also dried herbs to make them last a long time. You can grow herbs just for fun, for their taste, or their good smell.

◀ *Herbs are found in all kinds of different products.*

Clues in a Name

There are hundreds of herbs in the world. One herb **family** can include many similar but different herbs. The mint family (named *mentha*) includes chocolate mint, peppermint, spearmint, orange mint, apple mint, and dozens more.

The names of herbs sometimes describe what they look like or what they're used for. *Lamb's ear* has soft, furry silver leaves that look like lamb's ears. *Bedstraw* was used to stuff mattresses. **Herbalists** collected different plants to study them and see how they were alike or different. They grouped similar herbs into families. This study of herbs was the beginning of the science called **botany**.

Lavender is known for its nice smell and its beautiful color. ▶

Annuals and Perennials

There are two major kinds of herbs, **annuals** and **perennials**. Annuals live for just one season, or time of year, and then they die. Annual seeds need to be replanted each year. Perennials can live for many years, they bloom each year at the same time. Perennial herbs often grow very slowly. It's good to have a mix of annuals and perennials in your herb garden.

◀ Basil *is a perennial herb.*

What Plants Need

Where should you put an herb garden? Think of the things plants need to grow. Plants need sunshine. Most herbs need at least five hours of sun every day. Pick a sunny, flat place outside, away from shady trees or buildings. If you're growing your herbs in a pot inside, place them on a windowsill that gets a lot of sunshine.

Plants also need water. A plant's roots need water to draw **nutrients**, or food, up from the ground. Water helps carry the food up the stem to the leaves. Be sure to give the herbs enough water so the roots sink deep into the ground. The roots will reach down to drink. Deep roots keep the plant standing firmly.

Plants should be watered when the soil feels dry. ▶

Good Dirt

The third thing an herb needs to grow strong and healthy is fertile dirt, or dirt with enough nutrients to feed the plants. Perhaps it doesn't sound tasty to you, but plants love nutrients like **nitrogen** and **potassium**. You can buy **fertilizer** to make the dirt better for growing. Fertilizer is a mixture of chemicals that add to the dirt some of the nutrients herbs need. **Compost**, or decayed vegetables and plants, is the best fertilizer. Compost is also light and airy, so it makes it easy for plants to get water and for seeds and roots to grow strong. Sand and clay make dirt heavier, which makes it harder for herbs to get water.

◄ *This child is mixing soil with fertilizer to make good dirt for her herb plants.*

13

Mrs. Lee's Class

Mrs. Lee's class decided they wanted to grow an herb garden. They waited until spring, and then found a spot outside that was very sunny. First, they dug about 10 inches into the ground. Then they removed all the grass and stones from the dirt. Next, they added a little fertilizer so the dirt would be able to feed their herbs.

Students in Mrs. Lee's class dug about 10 inches into the ground to plant their herb garden. ▶

Planting the Herb Garden

Herb plants spread their own seeds in order to **reproduce**, but if you want to plant an herb garden, you have to buy the seeds or the plants themselves. Perennials are often sold as plants because they take a long time to grow. Seeds come in little packets that tell you how to grow the herbs. Mrs. Lee's class followed the directions on the seed packets and planted the herbs about one foot away from each other. This way the plants' roots and leaves would have enough room to grow, and food to eat.

The class wanted to grow some herbs that they could eat, so they planted *basil, dill, chives,* and *rosemary.* They also wanted to grow some sweet-smelling herbs, so they planted *lavender* and scented *geranium.*

◄ *Be sure to find out which herbs can be eaten and which can't before starting your garden.*

Listening to Leaves

After Mrs. Lee's class planted their seeds, the kids made sure that the soil stayed damp by watering the herbs on days that it didn't rain. Each day, someone poked a finger in the dirt to see if it felt dry. The class also watched the leaves. If the herbs' leaves drooped or got dry and crinkly, the class knew the herbs needed water. Sometimes, an herb can have too much water, though. If the leaves started to turn yellow, Mrs. Lee told the class not to water them.

You can help a plant grow by pulling off the yellow leaves. ▶

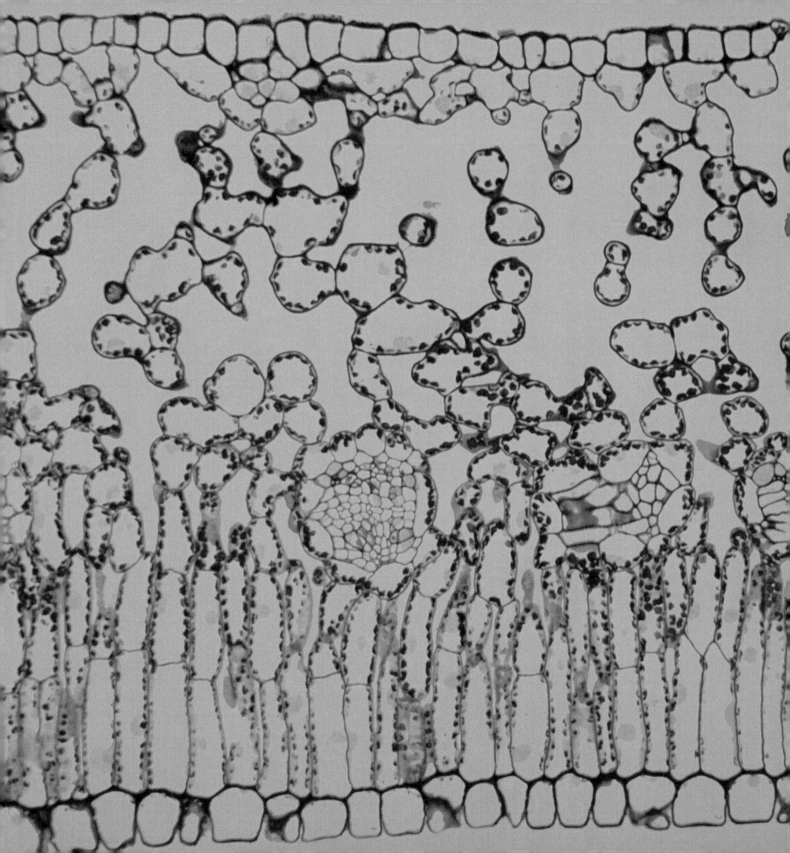

Photosynthesis

With sun, water, and good dirt, the class's herbs were ready to grow. Their leaves had something humans don't have: **chlorophyll**. Chlorophyll is what makes leaves green. The chlorophyll gets **energy** from the sunlight, and uses the energy to turn water, air, and nutrients into sugar. This process is called **photosynthesis**. Herbs then use the sugar as energy to grow and make their special tastes and scents.

Like people, seeds and plants have **genes**. Genes decide how the plant will look, smell, and taste. How the seed is planted, fed, and cared for, though, makes a big difference in how it grows.

Plant leaves have chlorophyll, which helps the plant soak up energy from the sun.

Using the Herbs

The class knew it was time to start picking when the herbs had grown big and leafy. Mrs. Lee showed them how to pick the leaves from the top of the plants. Some of the kids wanted to use the herbs to cook, so the class decided to use the **edible** herbs right away and dry the nice-smelling ones. This way they could use their herbs to make their homes smell pretty all through the winter. Edible herbs can be dried, too, and used for cooking. Mrs. Lee showed them how to dry the *geranium* and *lavender* by cutting the stems and hanging them upside-down in a dry, dark place. Then they each got to take some *basil, chives, dill,* and *rosemary* home to spice up their dinners!

Glossary

annuals (AN-yoo-alz) A plant that grows, blossoms, seeds, and dies in one season or year.

botany (BOT-uh-nee) The science or study of plants.

chlorophyll (KLOR-uh-fil) A green substance in leaves and plants.

compost (KOM-post) A mixture of decaying vegetables used as fertilizer to improve soil texture.

edible (ED-uh-bal) Fit to be eaten as food.

energy (EN-er-jee) The power to work or act. Plants need energy to grow.

family (FA-mih-lee) A group of herbs that are similar to each other.

fertilizer (FER-tih-ly-zur) Material like manure, compost, and chemicals added to dirt to make things grow.

genes (JEENZ) Any of several tiny parts joined together in a cell that make a living thing like its parents.

herbalists (UR-bul-ists) A person who collects herbs, especially medicinal herbs.

herbs (URBS) Plants that are used for medicine and seasoning.

nitrogen (NY-troh-jen) A chemical element that all living things need.

nutrients (NOO-tree-ents) A substance a living thing needs for energy to grow.

perennials (pur-EN-ee-uhlz) Plants that live three years or more and usually blossom after two years.

photosynthesis (fo-to-SIN-thih-sis) The process where carbon dioxide and water, in the presence of light and chlorophyll, are changed into sugar.

potassium (poh-TASS-ee-uhm) A chemical element plants need to grow.

reproduce (ree-proh-DOOS) To make more of the same of something.

Index

Web Sites:

You can learn more about growing herbs on the Internet. Check out this Web site: http://www.ext.vt.edu/pubs/envirohort/426-420/426-420.html